Ruth

30-DAY DEVOTIONAL

Ruth

Alistair Begg
with Elizabeth McQuoid

FOOD
FOR THE
JOURNEY

ivp

Keswick
Resources

INTER-VARSITY PRESS
36 Causton Street, London SW1P 4ST, England
Email: ivp@ivpbooks.com
Website: www.ivpbooks.com

First published 2017

British Library Cataloguing-in-Publication Data
A catalogue record for this book is available from the British Library.

ISBN: 978-1-78359-525-9
eBook ISBN: 978-1-78359-526-6

Typeset in Great Britain by CRB Associates, Potterhanworth, Lincolnshire
Printed in Great Britain by 4edge Limited, Essex

Preface

Can you guess how many sermons have been preached from the Keswick platform? Almost 6,500!

For over 140 years, the Keswick Convention in the English Lake District has welcomed gifted expositors from all over the world. The convention's archive is a treasure trove of sermons preached on every book of the Bible.

This series is an invitation to mine that treasure. It takes talks from the Bible Reading series given by well-loved Keswick speakers, past and present, and reformats them into daily devotionals. Where necessary, the language has been updated but, on the whole, it is the message you would have heard had you been listening in the tent on Skiddaw Street. Each day of the devotional ends with a newly written section designed to help you apply God's Word to your own life and situation.

Whether you are a convention regular or have never been to Keswick, this Food for the Journey series provides a unique opportunity to study the Scriptures with a Bible teacher by your side. Each book is designed to fit in your jacket pocket or handbag so you can read it anywhere – over the breakfast table, on the commute into work or college, while you are waiting in your car, during your lunch break or in bed at night. Wherever life's journey takes you, time in God's Word is vital nourishment for your spiritual journey.

Our prayer is that these devotionals become your daily feast, a precious opportunity to meet with God through his Word. Read, meditate, apply and pray through the Scriptures given for each day, and allow God's truths to take root and transform your life.

If these devotionals whet your appetite for more, there is a 'For further study' section at the end of each book. You can also visit our website at <www.keswickministries.org/resources> to find the full range of books, study guides, CDs, DVDs and mp3s available. Why not order an audio recording of the Bible Reading series to accompany your daily devotional?

Let the word of Christ dwell in you richly.
(Colossians 3:16, ESV)

Introduction
Ruth

Bad news.

Newspapers, social media, and TV bombard us with it constantly.

Is there any hope, any ray of light in the midst of this chaos?

We are not the first believers to have asked this question.

The story of Ruth takes place when the Israelites are living in the Promised Land after the death of Joshua. Instead of heeding the warnings God gave through Moses and Joshua, the people rebelled against God's rule. They served foreign gods, were taken over by their enemies and each time, in response to their cries for deliverance, God sent them a judge. 'But when the judge died, the people returned to ways even more corrupt than those of their ancestors, following other gods and serving and worshipping them. They refused to give up their evil practices and stubborn ways' (Judges 2:19). A vicious cycle ensued, and by the end of the book of Judges, brutality and immorality were commonplace: 'In those days Israel had no king; everyone did as they saw fit' (Judges 21:25).

It was into this whirl of social, religious and moral chaos that this book was written, reminding the children of God that there was hope; that a remnant of true faith remained; that God was continuing to work in the lives of ordinary people as they went about their daily chores.

The book takes our gaze off the heroes. There are no judges here, no Samson, no Gideon, no Jephthah, no amazing story of Rahab. Instead, God is preoccupied with a woman called Naomi. We are given an intimate glimpse into her family life and we witness, first hand, God's providence.

The book ends with a genealogy pointing forward to King David who was a 'man after God's heart', who would lead the people wisely. But it ultimately points us to Jesus, the great 'son of David' (Matthew 1:1) – the hope of the nations, the light of the world, the prince of peace.

Today, we see glimmers of hope and chinks of light breaking through the darkness. But chaos will prevail until Jesus returns to reign. In the meantime, don't lose heart. Be encouraged, for God is still preoccupied with people like Naomi. In the midst of everything that unfolds in life, in the mystery of his purpose, God sets his love and affection on unlikely people, in unlikely contexts, doing routine things. Quite surprisingly, he chooses to work his eternal purposes out in the ordinariness of the lives of ordinary people.

That includes you.

Day 1

Read Ruth 1:1–5
Key verse: Ruth 1:1

....

> ¹*In the days when the judges ruled, there was a famine in the land. So a man from Bethlehem in Judah, together with his wife and two sons, went to live for a while in the country of Moab.*

The result of a blood test, the loss of a loved one, a rash decision and life can unravel very quickly.

Here we find life falling apart in the space of five verses. The catalyst was a famine. God had warned his people that famine would be one of the consequences if they failed to obey his commands (Deuteronomy 32:24). The writer doesn't tell us how the famine came about. It could have been caused by the invasion of enemy forces or a drought. Whatever the cause, the famine is certainly the result of the providential dealings of God. It provides the backdrop for the story, introducing us to this little family of four.

When people heard the word 'famine', they knew that it had often proved to be a moment of great historical significance. 'There was a famine in the land', remember, and Abraham went down to Egypt to live there. 'There was a famine in the land' and Isaac went to Abimelech, the king of the Philistines. It was on account of famine in the land that Jacob and his sons ended up in Egypt. In each case, the famine proved to be pivotal, a turning point in the lives of the people of God as it was in the life of the young man in the story Jesus told in Luke 15.

Outsiders might have just thought, 'We're down on our crops' or 'It's exceptionally rainy', but God's children need to recognize that he is working things out in the very details of history according to the eternal counsel of his will. And in each case of famine, not least of all in this story, his servants were protected and provided for.

Is your life unravelling? It doesn't take much in the way of extra pressure, bad news, family strife or financial woes to feel as if life is fraying at the seams. Most of us are well acquainted with hardship. Suffering, in various guises, is part of our human experience. However, have you considered that this particular time of challenge in your life might be pivotal? A God-appointed time of spiritual growth, a crucial opportunity to exercise faith or develop deeper bonds of fellowship with other Christians? Don't waste your suffering. Don't waste your poor health, your unemployment, your financial struggles or your grief. However bleak the backdrop of your life, however difficult your present situation, seek God. Be open and ready to learn the lessons he wants to teach you in this season of your life.

Day 2

Read Ruth 1:1–5
Key verses: Ruth 1:1–2

....

¹In the days when the judges ruled, there was a famine in the land. So a man from Bethlehem in Judah, together with his wife and two sons, went to live for a while in the country of Moab. ²The man's name was Elimelek, his wife's name was Naomi, and the names of his two sons were Mahlon and Kilion. They were Ephrathites from Bethlehem, Judah. And they went to Moab and lived there.

Are you a decisive person? Many of us struggle with decision-making. When you don't know the outcome, when the future is uncertain, how can you be sure you are making the right decision?

Try to imagine Elimelek and his wife lying in bed chatting to each other before they fall asleep. He asks, 'What do you think we should do?' Naomi replies, 'What do you think God wants us to do?' Elimelek says, 'God wants us to use our brains. He wants us to be discriminating. He wants us to lean on our understanding.' Naomi says, 'Don't you think it might be good if we trusted in the Lord with all our hearts and trusted him with this famine? Shouldn't we trust him to direct our paths?' Elimelek sighs and rolls over: 'I'm going to sleep.' The next morning, he announces to his family that they are leaving to go to Moab.

The author doesn't criticize Elimelek's decision. In one sense it was understandable – he's supposed to provide for his family and he had the means to move to a better place. But from another perspective, it is astonishing. The family are living in Bethlehem, which means 'the house of bread'. Elimelek's own name means 'My God is king'; he knows that God's people are to be in God's place if they are going to live under God's rule and blessing. He also knows that the people of Moab are on the list of those with whom the people of God should not associate. Yet he still goes.

All of us, if we are honest, have made decisions and then thought, 'Maybe if I had the chance again, I would do that differently.' But the wonderful thing is that through it all and over it all, God remains in control.

You may be living with the consequences of bad decisions; most of us are. But don't bow to Satan's pressure to keep raking over them. Jesus' death on the cross has paid for your sins and wiped the slate clean. You are forgiven and God looks at you clothed with the righteousness of Christ. Whatever poor choices you have made in the past, God is still in control. He does not waste any of your tears or suffering, but uses it for your good and his glory.

Moving forward, resist the urge to do just whatever seems right to you. If you have decisions to make, bring them before God. Pray, ask for wisdom, listen to God speaking through his Word and, if it is appropriate, ask the advice of mature believers who know you well.

Bring these words from Proverbs to bear on your situation:

> Trust in the Lord with all your heart
>   and lean not on your own understanding;
> in all your ways submit to him,
>   and he will make your paths straight.
> (Proverbs 3:5–6)

Day 3

Read Ruth 1:1–5
Key verse: Ruth 1:2

....

> ² *The man's name was Elimelek, his wife's name was Naomi, and the names of his two sons were Mahlon and Kilion. They were Ephrathites from Bethlehem, Judah. And they went to Moab and lived there.*

When they were younger, my children used to love hearing what their names meant and why we chose them.

The fact that these verses are so full of names indicates the importance of what is going on here. As the story unfolds, we'll see that each name carries special significance in the purposes of God.

Elimelek's name means 'My God is king'. That's interesting! If he knows the Lord really is king – and therefore faithful and trustworthy – then why is he leaving Bethlehem? It caused quite a stir when Naomi returned to Bethlehem with Ruth (Ruth 1:19), so we can assume that it caused a stir when the family left. They were Ephrathites, an important clan, probably one of the more wealthy families. So everyone noticed what they did and that Elimelek failed to live up to his name.

Naomi's name means 'lovely', 'pleasant', 'delightful'. This is significant because of all the bitterness she will experience through losing her husband and two sons.

The boys' names, Mahlon and Kilion, come from two Hebrew words. We might call them 'sickly' and 'pining'. A clue as to what will happen to them!

Names are significant, and throughout this story we shall see God living up to his name and remaining true to his covenant promises.

Many of us are named after someone – perhaps a family member or a celebrity whom our parents admired. Often a name has special connotations for the person who chooses it.

God's name also has special significance; it represents the sum total of his character and power. The Bible often talks about the significance of the name of God:

> The name of the Lord is a fortified tower;
>   the righteous run to it and are safe.
> (Proverbs 18:10)

Some trust in chariots and some in horses,
    but we trust in the name of the LORD our God.
(Psalm 20:7)

Do not worship any other god, for the LORD, whose
name is Jealous, is a jealous God.
(Exodus 34:14)

No one is like you, LORD;
    you are great,
    and your name is mighty in power.
(Jeremiah 10:6)

Salvation is found in no one else, for there is no other
name under heaven given to mankind by which we must
be saved.
(Acts 4:12)

Today, meditate on the name of God and all that it
means. Surely, our only valid response is to say with
King David:

I will exalt you, my God the King;
    I will praise your name for ever and ever.
(Psalm 145:1)

Day 4

Read Ruth 1:1–5
Key verses: Ruth 1:3–5

....

> ³*Now Elimelek, Naomi's husband, died, and she
> was left with her two sons.* ⁴*They married Moabite
> women, one named Orpah and the other Ruth. After
> they had lived there about ten years,* ⁵*both Mahlon
> and Kilion also died, and Naomi was left without her
> two sons and her husband.*

Do you enjoy being the centre of attention? Some of us
like the limelight, while others prefer to blend into the
background.

If this story were a film, Naomi would certainly take centre
stage. Notice that the camera is on her a lot. Usually in
the Bible, the women are introduced in the light of the
men. Here the man is introduced in the light of his wife;
he is described as the husband of Naomi. This is interesting and purposeful.

Naomi is not only left without her husband, but then without her two sons. Of course they had married, and their marriages held the prospect of children coming along; however, not only were there no children born, but now the potential fathers were dead as well. As a result, the family name and the family's future were over. And the importance of the name for posterity's sake is at the heart of the culture of the people of God and at the very heart of this story. Naomi found herself absolutely hopeless and bereft – the family name had found itself in a cul-de-sac, and she was a lonely widow living as an alien in a male-dominated foreign place minus the protection and provision of a husband or sons.

So much is going on at this point in Israel's history, yet the focus of God is on a sad and lonely lady. This is the only book in the Bible entirely devoted to the domestic story of a woman. It shows the amazing compassion and empathy of God for the back streets and side alleys and the people who feel themselves to be last, lost and left out. God says, 'The whole world is going on, but I am with you. I hem you in behind and before. I have set my hand upon you.' That is the kind of God we worship.

God has got the whole world in his hands. That's true. But he also has you in the palm of his hands. God is sovereign over the affairs of state, international politics and the weather systems, yet he cares intimately and always for you. You may feel bereft like Naomi, with no silver lining to your circumstances, no way out, nothing to look forward to, but God's hand is upon you. As you bring your circumstances before God today, meditate and rest in the truth of David's words in Psalm 139:1–6.

You have searched me, LORD,
    and you know me.
You know when I sit and when I rise;
    you perceive my thoughts from afar.
You discern my going out and my lying down;
    you are familiar with all my ways.
Before a word is on my tongue
    you, LORD, know it completely.
You hem me in behind and before,
    and you lay your hand upon me.
Such knowledge is too wonderful for me,
    too lofty for me to attain.

Day 5

Read Ruth 1:1–5
Key verses: Ruth 1:3–5

....

> ³Now Elimelek, Naomi's husband, died, and she was left with her two sons. ⁴They married Moabite women, one named Orpah and the other Ruth. After they had lived there about ten years, ⁵both Mahlon and Kilion also died, and Naomi was left without her two sons and her husband.

What did the preacher promise you when you became a Christian? What did you expect from this new life of faith?

Look again at these opening verses of the book of Ruth. They serve as an antidote to the notion that the path of faith is strewn with rose petals. Neither the Bible nor human experience encourages us to think in this way.

In the course of verses 3–5, the family found the food that they so desperately needed, but they also faced circumstances which were dreadfully painful. No details are given, just the bald facts.

With the loss of her husband and two sons, Naomi had to grapple with God's providence in an intensely personal way. And as the drama unfolds, her view of the world remains firmly fixed on the God of Abraham, Isaac and Jacob. She doesn't regard herself as being held in the grip of some kind of blind impersonal force. Nor does she view her life as if she were a cork bobbing around on the ocean of chance.

Naomi would have been a Westminster Confession girl, describing God's providence as 'his most holy, wise and powerful preserving and governing of all his creatures and all their actions' (Westminster Shorter Catechism, 1674). Or with the theologian Berkhof she would have said, 'God's providence is the continued exercise of the divine energy whereby the Creator preserves all his creatures, is operative in all that comes to pass in the world and directs all things to their appointed end' (*Systematic Theology*, Banner of Truth Trust, 1971).

Naomi was going to discover, and has now discovered from the vantage point of eternity, that God was doing something far bigger than anything she could ever see. If you like, the story before us is a wonderful exposition of Romans 8:28. 'And we know that in all things God works for the good of those who love him, who have been called according to his purpose.'

What is the good that God is working towards? It is the separating out of a people and the transforming of a people into the likeness of his Son. He does use famine. He does use failure. He does use the silly, obviously bad things we do, in order to accomplish his final strategy for us.

Don't be surprised or knocked off course when you face difficulties. Trust in God's providence. In your struggles, unanswered questions and grief, know that 'every detail in our lives of love for God is worked into something good' (Romans 8:28, MSG). Or as William Cowper the hymn writer wrote,

Judge not the Lord by feeble sense,
But trust Him for His grace;
Behind a frowning providence
He hides a smiling face.
His purposes will ripen fast,
Unfolding every hour;
The bud may have a bitter taste,
But sweet will be the flower.
('God Moves in a Mysterious Way', 1774)

Day 6

Read Ruth 1:6–9
Key verses: Ruth 1:6–7

....

6When Naomi heard in Moab that the LORD had come to the aid of his people by providing food for them, she and her daughters-in-law prepared to return home from there. 7With her two daughters-in-law she left the place where she had been living and set out on the road that would take them back to the land of Judah.

When you are away from home, do you like to keep in touch?

Naomi, an alien living in a foreign place, obviously kept in touch with her homeland. She is a bit like Nehemiah, who was constantly hearing news about the state of Jerusalem when he was in Susa. One day, news reached Naomi in Moab that the Lord had come to the aid of his people. Or, as one translation puts it, 'The LORD had visited his people' (ESV).

On this occasion, he had come to their aid by providing food. We shouldn't miss the simplicity of this statement. When you live in the world of Asda or Tesco, it is possible to forget that God is the provider of everything we have. He makes the rain fall and the sun shine and so on. That is why it is imperative for us to make sure we don't get to the point in our Christian lives where saying grace is perfunctory. We need to guard against taking things, even ordinary things, for granted. Instead we should recognize God's provision and care each day.

Through the poor, painful tears of Naomi's disappointment, the sun shines in, the news comes and she could testify to Calvin's wise words – 'It is an absurd folly that miserable men take upon themselves to act without God when they cannot even speak except he wills' (*Institutes of the Christian Religion*, Hendrickson Publishers Inc., 2007).

- Today open your eyes, pause, and take stock of all the instances of God's grace and favour on your life.

- Practise being thankful for his care and provision in the big as well as the small things – the clothes you have to wear, the smile on your child's face, or the words of encouragement someone gave you.

- Start to see God's fingerprints all over your life – you arrived at work today not because the train was on time but because God protected you on your journey; there is food on your table not because you did an online shop but because God provided the rain and sun to grow the crops; you got a job not because you passed exams but because God gave you skills and enabled you to use them; you were able to care for a sick loved one today not because you are kind and patient but because God gave you his strength and compassion.
- Worship *Jehovah Jireh* – the God who provides.

Day 7

Read Ruth 1:6–10
Key verses: Ruth 1:8–9

....

> [8] Then Naomi said to her two daughters-in-law, 'Go back, each of you, to your mother's home. May the LORD show you kindness, as you have shown kindness to your dead husbands and to me. [9] May the LORD grant that each of you will find rest in the home of another husband.'
>
> Then she kissed them goodbye and they wept aloud.

We learn a lot if we listen.

Of the eighty-five verses in this book, fifty of them are dialogue. These conversations reveal a jumble of expectations, emotions, affirmations and misgivings.

The provision of food means that Naomi and her two daughters-in-law prepare to head to Judah (verse 6). And at some point along the road, this dialogue takes place.

Naomi says goodbye to Ruth and Orpah, and tries to persuade them to return to Moab.

You can picture the raw emotion of the scene. The three women wrapped in each other's arms, weeping together, Naomi pleading with the younger women to leave and them clinging to her.

Some commentators are convinced that Naomi was wrong to urge the girls to return to Moab. They suggest she was concerned about how it would look if she turned up in Bethlehem with these two foreigners. It would certainly highlight the fact that not only had her family lived among the people of Moab, they had gone one step beyond and married their inhabitants. These commentators portray Naomi as a selfish, cantankerous, bitter old lady.

However, the language of verses 8–9 suggests that Naomi's concern is prayerful and God-centred. She is not concerned about her own well-being but with their well-being and security – a security that is ultimately found in Yahweh but is, in the immediate term, expressed in their mothers' homes and in a husband's embrace.

There is a selflessness here about Naomi as she kisses her daughters-in-law and asks the Lord to show them kindness. The word is *hesed*, God's covenant love. She is commending them ultimately into the care of God. What else can we do for our children and those near and dear to us? The covenant love of God, says Alec Motyer, 'is that wonderful love that combines the warmth of God's fellowship with the security of God's faithfulness'.

Life is full of tearful goodbyes – a boyfriend or girlfriend moving to a different city for work or study; children growing up and leaving home; loved ones dying. Goodbyes of the temporary and more permanent kind are part and parcel of real life. When we are apart from friends and family, there is often little we can do to help them with their daily lives and struggles. One thing – the best thing – we can do is commend them to the covenant love of God. Though we cannot be with them, God's faithfulness will never leave them. As Psalm 121 promises:

> I lift up my eyes to the mountains –
>   where does my help come from?
> My help comes from the LORD,
>   the Maker of heaven and earth.
>
> He will not let your foot slip –
>   he who watches over you will not slumber;
> indeed, he who watches over Israel
>   will neither slumber nor sleep.

The Lord watches over you –
    the Lord is your shade at your right hand;
the sun will not harm you by day,
    nor the moon by night.

The Lord will keep you from all harm –
    he will watch over your life;
the Lord will watch over your coming and going
    both now and forevermore.

Day 8

Read Ruth 1:8–13
Key verses: Ruth 1:11–13

....

> [11] But Naomi said, 'Return home, my daughters. Why would you come with me? Am I going to have any more sons, who could become your husbands? [12] Return home, my daughters; I am too old to have another husband. Even if I thought there was still hope for me – even if I had a husband tonight and then gave birth to sons – [13] would you wait until they grew up? Would you remain unmarried for them? No, my daughters. It is more bitter for me than for you, because the Lord's hand has turned against me!'

Perhaps Naomi thought she'd persuaded her daughters-in-law to return home. She hears them saying, 'We will go back.' But then they add, 'with you to your people' (verse 10). And so Naomi launches into a little speech in verse 11, urging them to be sensible.

Her comments may seem strange, but she is referring to the custom of levirate marriage where if a man died childless, his brother was supposed to marry the widow to produce heirs to continue the family line. Naomi is saying this can't happen – even if she conceived tonight, Orpah and Ruth would be too old by the time the boys became men.

Apparently Naomi was perfectly prepared to believe that God was king over the affairs of her daughters-in-law, even if they were to go back into enemy territory. But when she thinks about her own circumstances, she can only see old age and loneliness beckoning. She recognizes that Ruth and Orpah have lost their husbands and are therefore not free from grief, but adds: 'It is more bitter for me than for you, because the LORD's hand has turned against me!'

Notice her theology. She is not saying, 'God turned his back and everything went wrong' or 'God is as surprised by this as I am.' She is not suggesting that the affairs of life are out of control. She affirms God's sovereign control, in that he brings to pass all that he wills. Hubbard says of her statement, 'Here we have bitter complaint cloaked in firm faith' (*The Book of Ruth*, Eerdmans, 1995). She recognizes that famine, exile, bereavement and childlessness have all proved to be in God's will for her.

Naomi is a good reminder to us that God is too wise to make mistakes; he is too kind to be cruel.

The commentator Atkinson describes faith not as a still light but like a mobile above a baby's cot. Imagine the image. When you hang a mobile in a child's room, at times one of the characters or pieces will be in the shadows, and then, as it moves around, it will come out into the sunshine. This is the life of faith for a believer.

Is your life in the light or the shadows? If you are crying out in bitter complaint, know that you are not alone. Believers like Naomi, the prophets Isaiah and Jeremiah, David in the Psalms, and even Jesus in Gethsemane cried out to God. Like them, will you hold firmly on to faith, trusting that our God is too wise to make mistakes, too kind to be cruel?

Day 9

Read Ruth 1:11–18
Key verses: Ruth 1:14–15

•••

¹⁴At this they wept aloud again. Then Orpah kissed her mother-in-law goodbye, but Ruth clung to her.
¹⁵'Look,' said Naomi, 'your sister-in-law is going back to her people and her gods. Go back with her.'

Do you wear your heart on your sleeve? Do you appreciate talking about your feelings? Or are the emotions of this story already exhausting you?

No-one needs to guess how these women are feeling. Their weeping, kissing and clinging make it blatantly obvious. When Naomi finishes her little speech, once again it is tears. Verse 14: 'At this they wept aloud again.' We have this whole scene acted out by the side of the road as back and forth these women cry, kiss and say goodbye.

Then the great divide comes. 'Then Orpah kissed her mother-in-law goodbye.' This was the final exchange of kisses and goodbyes. It was a defining moment. Orpah decided to be obedient to Naomi, to make the sensible choice.

What are we to make of this? Can we fault her for doing what Naomi urged? Is she walking away from the Living God? Is this an illustration of a borrowed faith that she decides not to make her own in the moment of opportunity? Or is it possibly an illustration of someone who decided to return to alien territory to live under the shadow of Yahweh's protection? I don't know and neither do you.

One day in heaven we can say, 'Excuse me, has anyone seen Orpah? I was looking for her because I don't know what happened on that roadway. I don't know if she was saved.' Wouldn't it be tremendous if Orpah's reasoning was: 'Naomi, you have convinced me so much that Yahweh is my protector and my provider that I will go back into that alien environment and under the shadow of his wings I will rest secure'?

One day, after a lifetime of kisses and tears, it will be our final goodbye. We don't know which goodbye will be our last, so we should make each conversation, each opportunity for the gospel count.

You may never know the impact your life had on the people in the Alpha/Christianity Explored course, the prodigal who had wandered from the faith, the mum at the school gate or the colleague in the office. Imagine if, as well as Orpah, there were people in heaven because you had spoken to them about Jesus? In the raw emotion of everyday life – the hellos and goodbyes, the tears and the laughter, the joys and the sadness – live out your faith. Let people see you trusting God in good times and bad. Pray that your life would be like a signpost pointing other people to God.

Day 10

Read Ruth 1:11–18
Key verses: Ruth 1:16–18

....

16 But Ruth replied, 'Don't urge me to leave you or to turn back from you. Where you go I will go, and where you stay I will stay. Your people will be my people and your God my God. 17 Where you die I will die, and there I will be buried. May the LORD deal with me, be it ever so severely, if even death separates you and me.' 18 When Naomi realised that Ruth was determined to go with her, she stopped urging her.

These verses are often quoted at weddings. But we shouldn't miss their deeper, more profound significance.

The cast is dwindling – there are only two left. Elimelek, Kilion and Mahlon didn't have speaking parts. So far, Naomi has been doing all the talking. Orpah's brief response provides the velvet from the jeweller's store, on which the diamond, this remarkable opening statement of Ruth's, shines.

Orpah is still in the distance; she isn't quite round the bend. Naomi urges Ruth to catch up with her, to go while she still has a chance. Ruth's eyes are following Orpah, but her hands are clinging to Naomi. Her heart is pulling her all over the place, her mind is formulating this little speech, and the radical decision she makes reverberates throughout redemption history.

It is fascinating that the same fact that caused Orpah to return caused Ruth to stay. Orpah processed Naomi's childlessness and decided that she would leave, desiring to become a wife. Ruth processed the information and decided that she would stay, committed to being a daughter. The same circumstances, the same information, a momentous decision: 'Wherever you go, I'm there.'

Ruth wasn't just agreeing to go on a short-term mission project. Her statement means goodbye to Orpah, goodbye to familiarity, goodbye to everything that has meant security to her, and hello to the great unknown. She was choosing an uncertain future as a widow in a land where she knew no-one. She was agreeing to stay with Naomi, 'till death do us part'. Even in death she promises to be buried with Naomi's people; that's a huge commitment. And her deep conviction came not only because of Naomi herself, but also on account of Naomi's God.

God is still looking for people of deep conviction, those who will nurture a 'till death do us part' kind of commitment.

Can you say these words to Christ?

'I'm committed to you through thick and thin. Where you go, I'll go. What you do, I'll do. Whom you love, I will love. I'm with you not only to death but through death.'

Perhaps, like Ruth, you need to leave something or someone behind to follow Christ. There will be sacrifices; the journey of faith is costly. Even today, your commitment to God will be challenged and tested. But hold on to God, persevere in your faith and don't be afraid to love him wholeheartedly. Because, like Ruth, you know what kind of God he is.

Day 11

Read Ruth 1:15–22
Key verses: Ruth 1:19–21

....

¹⁹ *So the two women went on until they came to Bethlehem. When they arrived in Bethlehem, the whole town was stirred because of them, and the women exclaimed, 'Can this be Naomi?'*

²⁰ *'Don't call me Naomi,' she told them. 'Call me Mara, because the Almighty has made my life very bitter.* ²¹ *I went away full, but the L*ORD *has brought me back empty. Why call me Naomi? The L*ORD *has afflicted me; the Almighty has brought misfortune upon me.'*

Village life doesn't lend itself to anonymity. If you have a baby, pass exams or even just change your bathroom suite, people tend to know about it!

Ruth and Naomi were never going to be able to slip into Bethlehem quietly. But perhaps even they were surprised at their reception. Women are nudging each other and saying, 'Is that Naomi? She's looking old, isn't she? Do you think she's lost weight? What happened to the boys? Who's the girl she's with?' 'They say she's a daughter-in-law.' 'Really? I'm going to ask her.'

So a lady went up to her and said, 'Is this really you, Naomi?' And Naomi replied, 'That's my name but not my experience. El-Shaddai has taken me down a bitter path. Full I went away, empty he has brought me back.'

Again in this dialogue, Naomi's honesty is striking. No hiding her feelings, no pretending about her life, no attempt to sweep it all aside with a stiff upper lip. Presumably walking into the town and seeing the old familiar places brought back all kinds of memories. Maybe the quick sighting of a friend who's grown old, the glimpse of young men who were contemporaries of her boys and the paths she had walked on in the early days with Elimelek all combined to overwhelm her emotionally. But she deals with her pain theologically. She says, 'Oh God. You are Almighty One. Famine, bereavement, sadness and loneliness, yes. But you are the Almighty One, you are *El-Shaddai*. I can leave the explanations and the responsibilities with you.'

Take a deep breath and step back from your current situation. Stop searching for explanations, stop grappling with doubt, stop being side-tracked by other people's questions and opinions. Instead, focus on God. Write down all you know and have experienced of his character: he is all-powerful, all-present, all-knowing and all-sufficient.

Today, choose to rest in his love and faithfulness and say with Naomi, 'But you are the Almighty One, you are *El-Shaddai*. I can leave the explanations and the responsibilities with you.'

Day 12

Read Ruth 1:15–22
Key verse: Ruth 1:22

....

22 So Naomi returned from Moab accompanied by Ruth the Moabite, her daughter-in-law, arriving in Bethlehem as the barley harvest was beginning.

Have you ever watched a TV series, desperate to know the outcome, only for the finale to end on a cliff hanger?

After all the sadness and grief, chapter 1 ends with similar intrigue. Ruth and Naomi arrived in Bethlehem 'as the barley harvest was beginning'. Signs of life and hope are appearing, and Bethlehem is finally living up to its name.

If this story were a film, the background music for the first five verses would have been a lament, perhaps a lone piper. But now the sun is forcing its way through the clouds, it is shining through the fields of barley, there's the inkling of a new day. The music changes; the lament ends and the melody line picks up and more strings fill the background. When God is at work, even hopelessness may prove the passageway to fresh starts and new opportunities.

What chapter 1 eventually says to us is that he who is King of the nations has the affairs of the world under his control. The Lord God omnipotent reigns. It may not always seem so, but it is so and he who is King of the nations is also Lord of the ordinary. So don't miss the simple stuff – food on your table, companionship, tears, honest questions – and in it all, the awareness that God is sustaining and guiding his children until, at last, the darkness is dispelled. Because, ultimately, the goodbyes of this chapter prepare us for the goodbye of death, and we are waiting for the dawning of the bright and blessed of days, when we shall see Christ in all his fullness.

Can you imagine that day? When the darkness fades, the clouds split open and Christ returns in all his glory; when your grief pales into insignificance in the beauty of his presence; when hope gives place to sight and your tears are wiped away once and for all. You know the final scene, the grand finale, of God's redemption story, so don't be discouraged. You feel the loss of your health, job or loved one keenly, but have you ever considered it was meant to be that way, that the pain has purpose? Perhaps pain and grief are means God uses to train our eyes on the horizon, to keep us looking forward for that eternal hope, and to speed its coming.

> Praise be to the God and Father of our Lord Jesus Christ! In his great mercy he has given us new birth into a living hope through the resurrection of Jesus Christ from the dead, and into an inheritance that can never perish, spoil or fade. This inheritance is kept in heaven for you, who through faith are shielded by God's power until the coming of the salvation that is ready to be revealed in the last time.
>
> (1 Peter 1:3–5)

Day 13

Read Ruth 2:1–3
Key verse: Ruth 2:2

....

> ²*And Ruth the Moabite said to Naomi, 'Let me go to the fields and pick up the leftover grain behind anyone in whose eyes I find favour.'*

When we see someone huddled asleep in a shop doorway or begging on the streets, we are often quick to make assumptions. Usually, we are wide of the mark.

The same applies to Ruth and Naomi. These two women were not poverty stricken as a result of indolence. They were not back in Bethlehem because they had made poor choices, bad decisions and were lazy. They are commendable, particularly this girl Ruth.

We don't know when she formed the plan that now unfolds. We don't know whether she and Naomi talked about their poverty and Yahweh's care for the poor as they walked along the road to Bethlehem.

If they had that conversation, it obviously wasn't a theoretical one. What Ruth was to discover was that God's law, in keeping with his concern for the helpless, the poor and the sojourner, had long made provision for the needy. God stipulated that the poor were not to be exploited (Deuteronomy 24:14), but paid daily (Deuteronomy 24:15) and shown justice (Exodus 23:6). A year of jubilee was also instituted so that every seven years, the land was left unploughed and the poor could help themselves to food from it (Exodus 23:11).

We read about another of God's plans to help the poor in Leviticus 23:22:

> When you reap the harvest of your land, do not reap to the very edges of your field or gather the gleanings of your harvest. Leave them for the poor and for the foreigner residing among you. I am the LORD your God.

Picking up the leftover grain from the fields was how those on the margins of society survived. And perhaps it was the sights and sounds of the barley harvest that stirred Ruth into action.

Because God was concerned for the poor, he expected his people to be equally concerned. No matter how prosperous they were, they were to treat individuals like Ruth and Naomi with a compassion which was representative of the compassion of God.

What poverty looks like and how we alleviate it may have changed, but God's expectations of his people haven't.

We talk about 'compassion fatigue' as if the relentless media images of human suffering somehow make us immune to people's needs. Yes, the need is great and sometimes we wonder what difference our small contribution makes. But don't give up on compassion! Again and again, the Bible tells us that God is compassionate (Psalm 86:15) and we his people are to mirror his character and priorities. Compassion is faith in action; it sets us apart as Christ's followers and commends the gospel powerfully (John 13:35). 'Therefore, as God's chosen people, holy and dearly loved, clothe yourselves with compassion' (Colossians 3:12). Put on compassion today – don't leave home without it!

Day 14

Read Ruth 2:1–3
Key verse: Ruth 2:2

....

²And Ruth the Moabite said to Naomi, 'Let me go to the fields and pick up the leftover grain behind anyone in whose eyes I find favour.'

Can you imagine Ruth's thoughts as she woke up that first morning in Bethlehem?

No doubt her heart and mind would have been flooded with all kinds of cares and concerns. But instead of lying in bed wallowing in self-pity, Ruth gets up and says to Naomi, 'Let me go to the fields and pick up the leftover grain behind anyone in whose eyes I find favour.'

Let's look again at the importance of this verse. Ruth doesn't look at her mother-in-law and say, 'What am I supposed to do now?' or worse still, 'So, what have you got planned for me, Naomi? This is where you live; I am not from here.' Nor does she suggest that it is time for

Naomi to get up and start working. No, she goes out on a limb. She risks being ostracized as a foreigner, perhaps even being harmed in the company of the workers. In this she provides a wonderful illustration of a principle that is increasingly absent in our culture: care for the elderly. We need to care for those who have invested their lives in us, who nurtured us and who, in many cases, now find themselves living in poverty or isolation. Any of us who are tempted to give short shrift to the notion of honouring our fathers and mothers, and our extended responsibilities to aunts and uncles, can certainly derive no support from the example of Ruth.

The initiative of Ruth is not only attractive but definitely instructive. Up in the morning, she's out to do what she can do. She knows that God will provide, but she knows that he does not routinely provide in a vacuum. She knows that God is sovereign, but she is coming to understand that his sovereignty takes into account her decisions and endeavours.

She walks out in the morning aware of the fact that what she needs more than anything is grace and favour.

No doubt you have heard the story about the man who, when out walking, fell down the side of a cliff. He cried out to God to save him. When the lifeboat came he refused to jump in, when the rescue helicopter came and lowered down a rope he didn't grab on to it; instead he believed that God would save him. The point is, of course, that God rarely works in a vacuum. He expects us to use the means at our disposal, exercise initiative and work hard. All the time trusting in his sovereignty and seeking his grace and favour. Consider your own situation. What resources and support has God provided? In what ways could you be taking initiative and working hard? Take action today, and at each step seek God's grace and favour.

Day 15

Read Ruth 2:1–3
Key verses: Ruth 2:1, 3

....

[1] *Now Naomi had a relative on her husband's side, a man of standing from the clan of Elimelek, whose name was Boaz . . .*

[3] *So [Ruth] went out, entered a field and began to glean behind the harvesters. As it turned out, she was working in a field belonging to Boaz, who was from the clan of Elimelek.*

'It just happened!' That's a cry we often hear from our children when they have had an accident or got into some kind of trouble.

And it just happened that Ruth ended up working in Boaz's field.

With a very light touch, the author has introduced us to Boaz in verse 1. He is a relation in Elimelek's clan and 'a man of standing'. He was a man whose influence wasn't tied only to his financial resources (which were to become apparent), but also to his moral integrity.

And amazingly Ruth finds herself in Boaz's field. What were the chances of that? There wasn't a big sign that said 'Boaz's field'. In fact, the vast acreage would have been divided up into allotments and everybody would have had their little bits and pieces. The owners knew where they were, but a stranger wouldn't have known whose field was whose. Ruth just launches into the first field she can. The King James Version of verse 3 is: 'Her hap was to light on a part of the field belonging unto Boaz.' It just happened that way. She could have gone somewhere else, but she went there.

One of the things it is important for us to hold on to is the fact that God overrules the freedom of our choices. Remember Joseph? His brothers were jealous, not because God made them jealous, but because they were bad rascals. They sold Joseph to Ishmaelite traders who transported him into captivity to sell him for a profit. The brothers were acting of their own volition. The Ishmaelites were acting of their own volition. And what was God doing? All of this, in the freedom of their choice, he was using according to the eternal counsel of his will to ensure that Joseph would be in Egypt to be able to provide for the very brothers who had disdained him with jealous hatred.

It is truly beyond our ability to comprehend. So what we should do is put our hands over our mouths and bow before God.

How the sovereignty of God and the freedom of human choice interface is a mystery. But we must hold these truths in tension and remember: 'What is before us? We know not whether we shall live or die but this we know, that all things are ordered and sure. Everything is ordered with an unerring wisdom and unbounded love, by Thee O God, who art love' (Charles Simeon, 1759–1836).

Don't say, 'It just happened.' Today, look out for God's guidance and the means he uses to order your path. Recognize and rejoice in divine coincidences.

Day 16

Read Ruth 2:1–7
Key verses: Ruth 2:4–5

....

> ⁴ *Just then Boaz arrived from Bethlehem and greeted the harvesters, 'The Lᴏʀᴅ be with you!'*
> *'The Lᴏʀᴅ bless you!' they answered.*
> ⁵ *Boaz asked the overseer of his harvesters, 'Who does that young woman belong to?'*

If you work in an office, factory or lab, does the atmosphere change when the boss arrives? If you are the boss, do you notice your employees shuffling uncomfortably or shutting down conversations when you appear?

Notice what happens when Boaz arrives on the scene in Bethlehem. He greets his workers with a blessing, 'The Lᴏʀᴅ be with you' and they call back, 'The Lᴏʀᴅ bless you!' These were not formulaic greetings but expressed Boaz's godly character, his kindness to his employees and their appreciation of him. What a wonderful place to work!

Boaz clearly knew his workers well. He immediately spots the new girl working in his field and asks his foreman about her. Interestingly, the man responds by giving him a detailed and honest report, underlining their effective working relationship.

This story does have something to say about the importance of employer–employee relationships. If you are a boss, you have a huge responsibility for the way in which you behave among your people. Likewise, how employees respond is also of great significance.

How does your work life – whatever that looks like for you – reflect your love for God?

If you go to work, you have a ready-made mission field. Many of us rub shoulders with the same people for more than eight hours every day – what an opportunity to be salt and light, pointing people to Jesus (Matthew 5:3–16). How we work, how we treat people, the values we promote – all of it – can be used by God to commend the gospel.

Whether you are the boss, the lowest employee in the organization or a volunteer for a charity, remember that you are ultimately serving your heavenly master, so 'whatever you do, whether in word or deed, do it all in the name of the Lord Jesus, giving thanks to God the Father through him' (Colossians 3:17).

Consider how Paul's words apply to you:

Servants, do what you're told by your earthly masters. And don't just do the minimum that will get you by. Do your best. Work from the heart for your real Master, for God, confident that you'll get paid in full when you come into your inheritance. Keep in mind always that the ultimate Master you're serving is Christ. The sullen servant who does shoddy work will be held responsible. Being a follower of Jesus doesn't cover up bad work.

And masters, treat your servants considerately. Be fair with them. Don't forget for a minute that you, too, serve a Master – God in heaven.

(Colossians 3:22 – 4:1, MSG)

Day 17

Read Ruth 2:4–10
Key verses: Ruth 2:8–10

....

[8] So Boaz said to Ruth, 'My daughter, listen to me. Don't go and glean in another field and don't go away from here. Stay here with the women who work for me. [9] Watch the field where the men are harvesting, and follow along after the women. I have told the men not to lay a hand on you. And whenever you are thirsty, go and get a drink from the water jars the men have filled.'

[10] At this, she bowed down with her face to the ground. She asked him, 'Why have I found such favour in your eyes that you notice me – a foreigner?'

Sometimes we are actually quite surprised when God answers our prayer requests.

It had been a matter of hours since Ruth had left Naomi. Her last words to her mother-in-law were, 'Let me go and find favour.' And now, in verse 10, she bows before Boaz and asks, 'Why have I found such favour?'

Boaz has noticed her in the field; he has heard about her background, humility and hard work, and introduces himself. He says, 'I don't want you to go anywhere else. Stay in my fields. Follow along with the girls. You'll be safe here.' Ruth's response in verse 10 indicates the tenderness which must have marked his directives, because she bowed her face to the ground in humility. The hopes of the morning have more than been fulfilled. The circumstances were way beyond what she could have asked or even imagined.

We don't find Ruth congratulating herself on her endeavours or for picking out the right field in which to work. She knew she just 'happened' to be there. Furthermore, she was a foreigner. She had worshipped other gods and would still be doing so if not for the intervention of the God of Abraham, Isaac and Jacob in her life when she met Naomi's family. As Ruth reflects on this light that has shone into her darkness, it is thankfulness and humility that are expressed in her very posture. Thankful people are humble and humble people are thankful; these traits sleep in the same double bed!

Ruth's question ought to be on the lips of every believer, when we come before the one who has made provision for us and under whose protective custody we live: 'Why have I found such favour?'

When you stop to think about it, examples of God's favour on your life are endless. But today, spend time thanking him for his great gift of salvation:

Remember that at that time you were separate from Christ, excluded from citizenship in Israel and foreigners to the covenants of the promise, without hope and without God in the world. But now in Christ Jesus you who once were far away have been brought near by the blood of Christ.
(Ephesians 2:12–13)

Day 18

Read Ruth 2:11–16
Key verses: Ruth 2:13–16

....

[13] *'May I continue to find favour in your eyes, my lord,' she said. 'You have put me at ease by speaking kindly to your servant – though I do not have the standing of one of your servants.'*

[14] *At mealtime Boaz said to her, 'Come over here. Have some bread and dip it in the wine vinegar.'*

When she sat down with the harvesters, he offered her some roasted grain. She ate all she wanted and had some left over. [15] *As she got up to glean, Boaz gave orders to his men, 'Let her gather among the sheaves and don't reprimand her.* [16] *Even pull out some stalks for her from the bundles and leave them for her to pick up, and don't rebuke her.'*

Who or what are you taking refuge in?

We don't like to admit it, but all of us take refuge in something; we seek security and protection in our job, family, reputation, even money.

The distinguishing feature of Ruth's life was that her refuge was in Yahweh.

Boaz has noticed Ruth's kindness to Naomi so he prays for her, in verse 12: 'May the LORD richly repay you for what you have done. May you be richly rewarded by the LORD, the God of Israel, under whose wings you have come to take refuge.'

In a sense, Boaz answers his own prayer by welcoming Ruth at the meal, offering her roasted grain and making sure she has enough to take home. Boaz points us forward to Jesus, the great provider, the one who intervenes in the lives of those who are poor, needy and alone.

Ruth's circumstances were uncomfortable, and yet Boaz spoke kindly to her (verse 13). She faced the possibility of antagonism, but he brought her under the jurisdiction of his protection, and so under the Lord's protection. And she was amazed by this – such comfort, such kindness. Especially as she didn't even have the standing of one of his servant girls. She is not thinking of entitlement. She regards the intervention of Boaz as an act of unmerited favour. She has no standing, but is brought into the protection and provision of a man of standing, who is prepared to give her all she needs and more.

Jesus is our man of standing, able to give us all we need and more.

Whatever your concerns or struggles, take refuge in Jesus today. He is your protector and provider; nestle in the shadow of his wings. He is the only one able to give you all you need – and so much more! Join the psalmist in praise:

How priceless is your unfailing love, O God!
    People take refuge in the shadow of your wings.
(Psalm 36:7)

Whoever dwells in the shelter of the Most High
    will rest in the shadow of the Almighty.
I will say of the LORD, 'He is my refuge and my fortress,
    my God, in whom I trust.'
(Psalm 91:1–2)

Day 19

Read Ruth 2:17–23
Key verses: Ruth 2:19, 22–23

....

¹⁹*Her mother-in-law asked her, 'Where did you glean today? Where did you work? Blessed be the man who took notice of you!'*

Then Ruth told her mother-in-law about the one at whose place she had been working. 'The name of the man I worked with today is Boaz,' she said . . .

²²*Naomi said to Ruth her daughter-in-law, 'It will be good for you, my daughter, to go with the women who work for him, because in someone else's field you might be harmed.'*

²³*So Ruth stayed close to the women of Boaz to glean until the barley and wheat harvests were finished. And she lived with her mother-in-law.*

I wish I could have been there to see Naomi's eyes when Ruth came along the road.

She'd sent her off in the morning with the general idea that she would glean in the fields. And when Ruth comes back, she can barely stand up with all the grain she's carrying. Then it is just as you'd imagine; all these questions. 'Where did you glean?' 'Where did you work?' Eventually, Ruth calmed Naomi down and told her all about her day.

These two women are committed to one another; their lives are woven together. Notice Ruth relaying all Boaz had said to her, and Naomi's motherly instinct in urging Ruth to stay in Boaz's field, where she would be protected. Ruth didn't reply, 'I'll do what I want, I don't need you.' No, she did what her mother-in-law said, gleaning until the barley and wheat harvests were finished.

And look how the chapter finishes: 'And she lived with her mother-in-law.' The author is not telling us about their living arrangements, but wanting us to notice how good it is that they loved each other. How good that they lived together in peace. How good that they discover together the provision of God. How wonderful that when their lives were so marked by poverty, they should be introduced to plenty. How fantastic that Naomi, Mrs Pleasant, who had been on such a bitter path, is being warmed up again by the sunshine of God's love.

Have you got a Ruth/Naomi relationship with anyone? Have you got someone you share life with, who celebrates God's grace with you and prays for you regularly? Most of us have good Christian friends, but will you take your friendship to a deeper level? Find ways to share your spiritual journey – pray together, share Bible verses or talk about the opportunities God is giving you at work or at home to live for him – and spur each other on to godliness.

As iron sharpens iron,
    so one person sharpens another.
(Proverbs 27:17)

Let us consider how we may spur one another on toward love and good deeds, not giving up meeting together, as some are in the habit of doing, but encouraging one another – and all the more as you see the Day approaching.
(Hebrews 10:24–25)

Day 20

Read Ruth 3:1–8
Key verses: Ruth 3:1–4

....

¹One day Ruth's mother-in-law Naomi said to her, 'My daughter, I must find a home for you, where you will be well provided for. ²Now Boaz, with whose women you have worked, is a relative of ours. Tonight he will be winnowing barley on the threshing floor. ³Wash, put on perfume, and get dressed in your best clothes. Then go down to the threshing floor, but don't let him know you are there until he has finished eating and drinking. ⁴When he lies down, note the place where he is lying. Then go and uncover his feet and lie down. He will tell you what to do.'

This scene should come with a warning: 'Don't try this at home'!

No mother today would suggest this as a plan of action for her daughter going off to college. But our social and cultural context is very different. Expectations, require-ments and obligations within marriage, courtship and interpersonal relationships were different on almost every level in twelfth-century BC Palestine.

Nevertheless, even in its time, this is an audacious plan. Naomi is trusting God and believing in the character of Boaz as she tries to arrange Ruth's marriage. Boaz is a man of standing, true, but he is still just a man, and the best of men are men at best. We could spend a long time reflecting on whether this was a good idea or not. You can perhaps imagine Ruth's eyes widening as Naomi explains the sheer bravado needed to implement this risky plan.

Having said that, while we may not be as ingenious as Naomi, we shouldn't overlook the privilege and responsi-bility of helping our young people find life partners. Today many thousands of people sign up to internet dating sites to find someone compatible with whom to spend their lives. This represents a crying need in our culture. So, if you are able, host meals and social events where, in the company of many others, singles can meet. Many of us can be thankful to friends who helped us in this way.

If only a marriage could be arranged by lying down at someone's feet! Relationships are complex. Even if, like Naomi, God prompts you to take action to pursue a relationship, prayer needs to be the bedrock.

- If you are divorced, bereaved or single, pray that your primary focus would be on God – now, and in any prospective relationship.
- If you are a parent, pray for your child's salvation. Pray that they would be faithful to God if they are called to singleness or marriage. Pray also for their prospective marriage partner – that God would keep them pure and devoted to him.
- If you are married, pray that your marriage would be God-centred and God-glorifying.

Day 21

Read Ruth 3:1–8
Key verses: Ruth 3:3–5

....

> [3] *Wash, put on perfume, and get dressed in your best clothes. Then go down to the threshing floor, but don't let him know you are there until he has finished eating and drinking.* [4] *When he lies down, note the place where he is lying. Then go and uncover his feet and lie down. He will tell you what to do.'*
>
> [5] *'I will do whatever you say,' Ruth answered.*

'I will do whatever you say.' Most parents would be thrilled to hear those words!

In chapter 1, Ruth showed her devotion to Naomi by not doing what she said, by not returning home to Moab. Here in chapter 3, she shows her devotion to Naomi by doing *exactly* what she said.

Naomi is following the Law of Moses. The law made provision for those who had become destitute as a result of the death of a spouse. When property had been sold in order to ease the poverty, God's law stipulated that a kinsman redeemer would purchase it to secure the property for the impoverished family. This also ensured that the land of Israel would remain within the families of Israel. In the same way, the brother or another close relative within the family would marry the widow in order to produce a child, so as to continue the family name. This is referred to as levirate marriage. As Boaz has been identified as a kinsman redeemer, it seems wise to Naomi to approach him.

Ruth understands exactly what this plan is about; it is not a fool's errand. She has her whole future ahead of her, but she is not thinking about herself or the type of man she would like to marry. She is thinking about what is best for Naomi. 'So she went down to the threshing floor and did everything her mother-in-law told her to do' (verse 6). But let's not romanticize this scene. There is nothing sexual or sensual about lying on the floor by a pile of grain. This is not an attractive proposition! It is obedience that takes Ruth there.

'I will do whatever you say.' If earthly parents are thrilled to hear those words, imagine how God, our heavenly Father, feels when we set aside our preferences and concerns, and determine to obey him wholeheartedly. Perhaps there is a command he is asking you to obey, a promise he wants you to cling to or a place he's sending you to. Will you obey him today, not because it suits you or benefits you in some way, but simply because it delights God's heart?

Day 22

Read Ruth 3:6–14
Key verses: Ruth 3:9–13

....

⁹ *'Who are you?' he asked.*

'I am your servant Ruth,' she said. 'Spread the corner of your garment over me, since you are a guardian-redeemer of our family.'

¹⁰ *'The LORD bless you, my daughter,' he replied. 'This kindness is greater than that which you showed earlier: you have not run after the younger men, whether rich or poor.* ¹¹ *And now, my daughter, don't be afraid. I will do for you all you ask. All the people of my town know that you are a woman of noble character.* ¹² *Although it is true that I am a guardian-redeemer of our family, there is another who is more closely related than I.* ¹³ *Stay here for the night, and in the morning if he wants to do his duty as your guardian-redeemer, good; let him redeem you. But if he is not willing, as surely as the LORD lives I will do it. Lie here until morning.'*

What do you think Ruth and Boaz looked like?

We may imagine Ruth to be very pretty and Boaz to be a distinguished older gentleman but, actually, we are never told. It is their characters, not their appearances, which are recorded.

'The mouth speaks what the heart is full of' (Matthew 12:34). Notice how quickly Boaz speaks about the Lord: 'The LORD bless you,' he says. He also expresses kindness to Ruth, calling her 'my daughter', a wonderful tenderness that acknowledges the significance of their age difference. He then commends her kindness to Naomi in leaving Moab. But he recognizes that this marriage proposal is taking kindness to a whole new level. Ruth could have married for love or for money, but the fact that she was on the threshing floor in the middle of the night, making this proposal on the strength of family loyalty, is an expression of *hesed* love. Ever since her arrival in Bethlehem, people have remarked on her noble character.

The pace of the story now slows right down, and into the drama comes the possibility that the marriage we have been holding our breath for might not happen. Boaz explains he would gladly marry Ruth, but there is a legal technicality: a kinsman redeemer closer than him. His honesty and integrity could put a stop to Naomi's plan. But Boaz's number one concern is, 'What is the right thing to do?' Even if the situation does not end up as they hope, Boaz is determined to do the right thing.

How would people describe you? Do your godly speech and choices get you noticed? Are you known for doing the right thing even if it costs you? Today:

- Be still and ask God to reveal the areas of your inner life you need to work on.
- Ask the Holy Spirit for help and opportunities to develop a godly character.
- Say 'no' to self and 'yes' to Christ's will.

Set this as a pattern each day, and your character will increasingly display the fruit of the Spirit (Galatians 5:22–23).

Day 23

Read Ruth 3:9–18
Key verses: Ruth 3:15–17

....

15[Boaz] also said, 'Bring me the shawl you are wearing and hold it out.' When she did so, he poured into it six measures of barley and placed the bundle on her. Then he went back to town.

16When Ruth came to her mother-in-law, Naomi asked, 'How did it go, my daughter?'

Then she told her everything Boaz had done for her 17 and added, 'He gave me these six measures of barley, saying, "Don't go back to your mother-in-law empty-handed."'

Why did Boaz give Ruth the barley?

Ruth's early morning adventures could have raised questions of inappropriate behaviour. But by carrying the barley, she looked as though she was just finishing the night shift.

Yet the gift of the barley was more than just a cover-up. Boaz's comment, 'Don't go back to your mother-in-law empty-handed', should remind us of Naomi's great statement in 1:21: 'I went away full, but the LORD has brought me back empty.'

There were two kinds of emptiness represented in the life of Naomi: the emptiness of childlessness and the emptiness of hunger as a result of famine. With the provision of this grain in amazing abundance, Boaz is saying to Naomi through Ruth, 'You can stop worrying about what you are going to eat; all that emptiness is dealt with.'

But the Hebrew text in 1:21 can also connote childlessness. If it can connote that in chapter 1, it can do so here as well. The grain is a suitable symbol of offspring to come. The commentator Hubbard says that 'the seed to fill the stomach was promise of the seed to fill the womb' (*The Book of Ruth*, Eerdmans, 1995). Ruth has arrived home with a bundle for her and Naomi to enjoy, and there is the prospect of the arrival of another little bundle in the near future!

This big bundle represents God's answer to the dilemma to which Naomi could see no answer when she left Moab. She had urged Orpah and Ruth to leave her because she had no future; she was empty, with no possibility of that emptiness being filled.

But as she listens to Ruth, she realizes that God is able to do exceedingly and abundantly beyond all she can ask or imagine.

God is the same yesterday, today and for ever (Hebrews 13:8). He is always caring and working on behalf of those who love him. If he could satisfy an empty, barren widow like Naomi, surely he can intervene in your situation. Stop letting worry dictate how you feel, stop trying to manipulate outcomes; instead determine to trust God with your circumstances. Look to him alone to fill and satisfy you. Put your hope in God, for 'he is able to do immeasurably more than all we ask or imagine' (Ephesians 3:20).

Day 24

Read Ruth 3:7–18

Key verses: Ruth 3:13–14, 16–18

....

¹³'Stay here for the night, and in the morning if he wants to do his duty as your guardian-redeemer, good; let him redeem you. But if he is not willing, as surely as the Lord lives I will do it. Lie here until morning.'

¹⁴ So she lay at his feet until morning, but got up before anyone could be recognised . . .

¹⁶When Ruth came to her mother-in-law, Naomi asked, 'How did it go, my daughter?'

Then she told her everything Boaz had done for her ¹⁷and added, 'He gave me these six measures of barley, saying, "Don't go back to your mother-in-law empty-handed."'

¹⁸Then Naomi said, 'Wait, my daughter, until you find out what happens. For the man will not rest until the matter is settled today.'

Are you a 'big picture' person or do you enjoy dealing with detail?

For a moment, look up from the details of this story and the everyday lives of these two women, and consider the bigger picture it is pointing to.

Naomi's ingenious plan has been carried out to perfection by Ruth. What Naomi prayed would be part and parcel of Ruth and Orpah's lives is about to be answered in a far more wonderful way than she could have conceived. In the freedom of the actions of these individuals, God's providence has been at work using even wrong or strange choices to conform everything to the eternal counsels of his will.

As we await the final instalment of the story, we see how Boaz points forward to the Lord Jesus. For Jesus Christ is our kinsman redeemer, becoming like us, identifying with us in every way and yet without sin. And when we, like Ruth, cast ourselves at the feet of Jesus, depending on his mercy, aware of the fact that we are outsiders, he grants forgiveness, he welcomes us with a steadfast love and he loads us down with his benefits. In the Lord Jesus we are granted one benefit after another. Boaz takes Ruth to himself, sharing his life and abundance with her. By redeeming us, Jesus makes us his bride; we have a Saviour to whom we may go and for whom we may live.

You are loaded down with benefits. It doesn't always feel like it, because sorrow and worry often cloud our focus. But today, remind yourself of this truth: rehearse God's blessings on your life, say them out loud, write them down. Physically and spiritually, bow at Jesus' feet, signalling your complete dependence on him for all things. And as the psalmist encourages us:

> Praise the LORD, my soul;
>   all my inmost being, praise his holy name.
> Praise the LORD, my soul,
>   and forget not all his benefits –
> who forgives all your sins
>   and heals all your diseases,
> who redeems your life from the pit
>   and crowns you with love and compassion,
> who satisfies your desires with good things
> so that your youth is renewed like the eagle's.
> (Psalm 103:1–5)

Day 25

Read Ruth 3:18 – 4:4
Key verses: Ruth 3:18 – 4:1

....

¹⁸ *Then Naomi said, 'Wait, my daughter, until you find out what happens. For the man will not rest until the matter is settled today.'*

^{4:1} Meanwhile Boaz went up to the town gate and sat down there just as the guardian-redeemer he had mentioned came along. Boaz said, 'Come over here, my friend, and sit down.' So he went over and sat down.

Standing in the queue at the supermarket checkout; biding your time until the doctor rings with your test results; being put on hold during a phone conversation. Waiting is part of life – we do a lot of it, but we don't like it.

At the end of chapter 3, Naomi issues the instruction to Ruth to 'Wait, until you find out what happens'. Like Naomi and Ruth, the readers are sitting on the edge of their seats. The resolution of this story apparently hinges on the response of an unknown character to this most important question.

Chapter 4 begins, 'Meanwhile Boaz went up to the town gate and sat down there.' There is a lot of sitting around at the end of chapter 3 and here at the beginning of chapter 4. But notice that Boaz is waiting with purpose. He is sitting in the public square, in the place where business was transacted and legal matters were settled, so that he can resolve this situation with the nearer kinsman redeemer. He puts himself in a position to meet this man if he happens to come along.

No doubt people travelling in the early morning to their places of work and to places of opportunity would have spoken to him on the way. Clearly Boaz knew it was a big day. It was a big day for him and for Ruth, but he could never have known the part he was playing in redemptive history.

Waiting is part of life – our physical and spiritual life. We wait for God to intervene in our situation, to answer prayers, to fulfil his purposes and for Jesus to return. But waiting does not mean inactivity. The Bible urges us to wait expectantly (Psalm 5:3), patiently (Psalm 37:7) and with hope (Psalm 33:20). Wait purposefully –

pray, use the time to grow as a disciple, be active serving God, be available for him to use. Don't begrudge the waiting – like Boaz and Ruth, you have no idea what God is doing behind the scenes and what part your waiting will play in God's plan of salvation.

I say to myself, 'The LORD is my portion;
    therefore I will wait for him.'
(Lamentations 3:24)

Day 26

Read Ruth 4:1–8
Key verses: Ruth 4:1–6

....

¹Meanwhile Boaz went up to the town gate and sat down there just as the guardian-redeemer he had mentioned came along. Boaz said, 'Come over here, my friend, and sit down.' So he went over and sat down.

²Boaz took ten of the elders of the town and said, 'Sit here,' and they did so. ³Then he said to the guardian-redeemer, 'Naomi, who has come back from Moab, is selling the piece of land that belonged to our relative Elimelek. ⁴I thought I should bring the matter to your attention and suggest that you buy it in the presence of these seated here and in the presence of the elders of my people. If you will redeem it, do so. But if you will not, tell me, so I will know. For no one has the right to do it except you, and I am next in line.'

'I will redeem it,' he said.

⁵*Then Boaz said, 'On the day you buy the land from Naomi, you also acquire Ruth the Moabite, the dead man's widow, in order to maintain the name of the dead with his property.'*

⁶*At this, the guardian-redeemer said, 'Then I cannot redeem it because I might endanger my own estate. You redeem it yourself. I cannot do it.'*

The man with no name.

In a story where names are significant, we are interestingly never told the kinsman redeemer's name. Boaz simply calls him over and invites him and the ten elders to sit down. He explains there is a property to buy belonging to Elimelek, and the man readily agrees to the purchase.

The audience gasps. This is not supposed to happen!

But Boaz adds, 'Before you take your sandal off to seal the deal, you should know that along with the land, you get a wife.' This is a different proposition altogether. If the kinsman redeemer were only required to buy the land, then, although he would pay the purchase price, he would still have an accruing asset. But if he took on a wife with the land and they had a child, the child would inherit the land. Therefore, it would be of no economic benefit to him. The heirs of the marriage might become part of the disbursement of his resources, and he didn't want to jeopardize his retirement strategy. So he declined to redeem the land.

Do you see the paradox? The one who is concerned about securing the rights to his family name is not remembered and the one who is selflessly concerned for the needs of others is, of course, remembered for his kindness.

Beware of trying to make a name for yourself. Like the builders of the tower of Babel, ultimately you will be frustrated (Genesis 11:1–9). Clinging on to your resources, your reputation, your 'name', is like trying to hold on to sand. But spend your energy promoting God's name like the woman who anointed Jesus' feet (Matthew 26:6–13) or the Israelite midwives, Shiphrah and Puah (Exodus 1:15–21), and you will be remembered for ever. What a paradox! Our names are only remembered when our sole aim is to make God's name great. Today, share John the Baptist's prayer: 'He must become greater; I must become less' (John 3:30).

Day 27

Read Ruth 4:9–12
Key verses: Ruth 4:11–12

. . . .

¹¹ *Then the elders and all the people at the gate said, 'We are witnesses. May the LORD make the woman who is coming into your home like Rachel and Leah, who together built up the family of Israel. May you have standing in Ephrathah and be famous in Bethlehem.*¹² *Through the offspring the LORD gives you by this young woman, may your family be like that of Perez, whom Tamar bore to Judah.'*

How do you celebrate good news? Perhaps you phone a friend, post on Facebook or go out for a special meal?

Look at how these well-wishers respond to this wedding announcement. As the details of the transaction are formalized, the crowd cheers in the grandstand. But it is not simply cheering; it is really a praying crowd.

The book has been full of prayers on the lips of all these different characters: 'May the Lord show kindness to you', 'May the Lord be with you', May the Lord repay you', 'May the Lord bless you', 'May the Lord grant you favour' and so on.

Now in verse 11 the elders, who have witnessed Boaz's acquisition of the land and a wife, begin to pray. They have seen Ruth's kindness to Naomi and also Boaz's commitment to this family. Notice Boaz's detailed and solemn statement in verse 10. He is well aware that he is marrying Ruth for the greater purpose of maintaining the name of the dead man's property.

As witnesses of such devotion, the elders pray, first for Ruth. They pray that she will be like Rachel and Leah, the founding mothers of Israel. Then they pray for Boaz: 'May you have standing in Ephrathah and be famous in Bethlehem.' Finally, they pray that this couple would have a family like Perez, who was also born of an outsider, and who became a clan chief in the nation.

These weren't pygmy prayers!

How would you describe your prayer life? Do you use prayer like an Aladdin's lamp, only speaking to God when you need something? Or are you like Daniel in the Old Testament, believing prayer is worth risking your life for? Most of us are somewhere in the middle of this spectrum, but you shouldn't settle for mediocrity. Determine to pray more; to pray more ambitiously and more biblically. Use one of Paul's prayers as you pray for friends and family today (see Ephesians 3:14–21, Philippians 1:9–11 and Colossians 1:9–14).

> Devote yourselves to prayer, being watchful and thankful.
> (Colossians 4:2)

Day 28

Read Ruth 4:9–13
Key verses: Ruth 4:13

. . . .

> ¹³ *So Boaz took Ruth and she became his wife. When he made love to her, the LORD enabled her to conceive, and she gave birth to a son.*

In verse 13, the story shifts from the boardroom to the bedroom.

As marriages crumble, as legal institutions seek to re-define it, as Christians lose their voice to address it because of pre-marital sex, extra-marital sex and total confusion in their minds, society hastens down a road on a fast train with apparently no driver. Therefore, when the Bible expresses God's concerns about marriage, we need to pay very careful attention.

'For this reason, a man will leave his father and mother and be united to his wife, and the two will become one flesh' (Ephesians 5:31). Marriage is not some arbitrary arrangement which has been conceived in a moment of time. It is not a contrivance of man. Marriage is a creation ordinance. God has designed and established it, and the order of things is vital: leaving, cleaving, being inter-woven and conceiving. To alter the structure is to bring chaos into our lives and into the life of society.

When the car drives away with the bride and groom, the people are supposed to watch them and say, 'When they come back they will be different.' The couple are sup-posed to go away on their honeymoon as virgins and come back having been physically united. Do you know how seldom that takes place, even within the Christian community? Why? Because people are disobedient. But if Jesus is Lord, then I am not at liberty to disbelieve what he teaches or demands of my behaviour.

Bonhoeffer said:

> Marriage is more than your love for each other. It has a higher dignity and power, for it is God's holy ordinance. . . In your love you only see the heaven of your happiness but in marriage you are placed at a post of responsibility towards the world and mankind.
> (*Letters and Papers from Prison*, Touchstone, 1997)

Your love is your own private possession, but marriage is something more than personal. It is a status; it is an office that joins you together in the sight of God and man. If the Christian church will not stand up for the nature of marriage, then no-one will. We must clean up our act and pray: 'Oh, that you would rend the heavens and come down' (Isaiah 64:1); judgment needs to start with the family of God (1 Peter 4:17).

- Unlike Ruth and Boaz, not all of us have obeyed God's divine order for love and marriage. Repent for past sin. Receive God's forgiveness and grace. From today onwards, serve God joyfully, knowing you are pure and holy in his sight, clothed in the righteousness of Christ.
- If you are married, pray for God's strength to maintain your marriage vows.
- Pray for the marriages of family and friends, that they would be God-honouring and a beacon of hope in our confused culture.

Day 29

Read Ruth 4:13–22
Key verses: Ruth 4:14–17

....

¹⁴ *The women said to Naomi: 'Praise be to the L*ORD*, who this day has not left you without a guardian-redeemer. May he become famous throughout Israel!* ¹⁵ *He will renew your life and sustain you in your old age. For your daughter-in-law, who loves you and who is better to you than seven sons, has given him birth.'*

¹⁶ *Then Naomi took the child in her arms and cared for him.* ¹⁷ *The women living there said, 'Naomi has a son!' And they named him Obed. He was the father of Jesse, the father of David.*

What a wonderful ending.

What a lovely picture: 'Then Naomi took the child in her arms and cared for him' (verse 16).

The film that began in black and white is now in glorious technicolour. The soundtrack that was a lament now swells to a triumphant crescendo, and Ruth, who hasn't had a speaking part since chapter 3:17, is now fading completely from view and the camera is back on Naomi.

All her concerns of chapter 1 have been more than answered in the providence of God. The women of the community gather together to remind Naomi how much her daughter-in-law loves her and is better to her than seven sons. They are delighted that this new baby will renew Naomi's life and sustain her in her old age.

Let this be an encouragement to every Naomi. Through experiences of bitterness and disappointment, God is at work and Naomi, who changed her name to Mara, is now very happy to be called Naomi again. Wonder of all wonders, miracle of miracles, the God of the nations who is vitally involved in the personal life of this widow and her daughter-in-law provides this little bundle that is now on her lap.

God is passionately preoccupied with Naomi – and all those ordinary people like her on the humdrum track of life.

When we face difficulties or go through suffering, it can be tempting to doubt God's love. No matter how long we've been a Christian or how often we have experienced God's faithfulness, we may question whether God hears our prayers and why he doesn't intervene. Today, refuse to believe the devil's lies. Acknowledge that God is passionately preoccupied with you. Let this truth sink deep into your heart.

God cares about all the issues you are facing, and he is providing for you in ways you cannot see. One day soon, in the new creation, the loose ends of life will be tied up and all of God's work behind the scenes will be on display. Until then, commit all the mundane elements of your life to God, trust his care for you and rest in the secure knowledge of his love.

Day 30

Read Ruth 4:13–22
Key verses: Ruth 4:18–22

....

¹⁸ *This, then, is the family line of Perez:*
   Perez was the father of Hezron,
   ¹⁹ *Hezron the father of Ram,*
   Ram the father of Amminadab,
   ²⁰ *Amminadab the father of Nahshon,*
   Nahshon the father of Salmon,
   ²¹ *Salmon the father of Boaz,*
   Boaz the father of Obed,
   ²² *Obed the father of Jesse,*
   and Jesse the father of David.

The whole story of the Bible is about getting from Genesis 12 to Revelation 7.

In Genesis 12, God calls Abraham to leave his people and his father's household and go to a land he does not know. God promises to make him into a great nation and bless all the peoples of the earth through him. In Revelation 7, we see the promise of God fulfilled when John sees a great multitude that no-one could count from every nation, tribe, people and language.

If you realize that we get to Revelation 7 as a result of the promise of God in Genesis 12, then you will begin to put the big picture together. Remember at the end of the book of Judges it says, 'In those days Israel had no king; everyone did as they saw fit' (Judges 21:25). The implication is that if Israel had a king, life would be so much better. Then you have this story of Ruth, which ends with the genealogy – and who is at the end? David, the shepherd boy who became king. David is a man after God's own heart, but he isn't perfect and when we watch his reign, we realize he doesn't totally fit the picture. He is clearly not the serpent-crusher who had been promised in Genesis 3. He is obviously not the great ruler from the tribe of Judah mentioned in Genesis 49. There is still one greater than David to come, which is made clear to him by Nathan the prophet. In 2 Samuel 7:12–16 are these amazing words that are partially fulfilled in Solomon and are ultimately fulfilled only in Jesus, who puts Solomon in the shadows (Luke 11:31).

This is how redemption history unfolds. Just when we think we have the fulfilment of God's promises, we realize they are only partially fulfilled. The story of Ruth points us forward to King David, but eventually we have to acknowledge that he is not the one we are waiting for. And so the story points us further forward, to a descendant of David: Jesus, our great kinsman redeemer. Ultimately we discover that these relatively unknown, apparently insignificant lives of Ruth and Boaz are central to all that God is doing in the world.

Jesus is coming back! That scene from Revelation 7 will soon take place. Be encouraged that the eternal significance of your relatively unknown, apparently insignificant life will soon be revealed. Until then, keep your focus on Christ – your kinsman redeemer and King. Determine how you should spend your day and what your priorities should be in the light of his imminent return.

For further study

If you would like to do further study on the book of Ruth, the following may be useful.

- Atkinson, David, *The Message of Ruth* (BST) (IVP, 1974)
- Ferguson, Sinclair, *Faithful God: An Exposition of the Book of Ruth* (Bryntirion Press, 2005)
- Hubbard, Robert, *The Book of Ruth* (NICOT) (Eerdmans, 1995)
- Piper, John, *A Sweet and Bitter Providence* (IVP, 2010)
- Younger, K. Lawson, *Judges/Ruth – NIV Application Commentary* (Zondervan, 2002)

KESWICK MINISTRIES

Our purpose

Keswick Ministries is committed to the spiritual renewal of God's people for his mission in the world.

God's purpose is to bring his blessing to all the nations of the world. That promise of blessing, which touches every aspect of human life, is ultimately fulfilled through the life, death, resurrection, ascension and future return of Christ. All of the people of God are called to participate in his missionary purposes, wherever he may place them. The central vision of *Keswick Ministries* is to see the people of God equipped, encouraged and refreshed to fulfil that calling, directed and guided by God's Word in the power of his Spirit, for the glory of his Son.

Our priorities

Keswick Ministries seeks to serve the local church through:

- *Hearing God's Word*: the Scriptures are the foundation for the church's life, growth and mission, and *Keswick Ministries* is committed to preaching and teaching God's Word in a way that is faithful to Scripture and relevant to Christians of all ages and backgrounds.

- *Becoming like God's Son*: from its earliest days the Keswick movement has encouraged Christians to live godly lives in the power of the Spirit, to grow in Christlikeness and to live under his lordship in every area of life. This is God's will for his people in every culture and generation.

- *Serving God's mission*: the authentic response to God's Word is obedience to his mission, and the inevitable result of Christlikeness is sacrificial service. *Keswick Ministries* seeks to encourage committed discipleship in family life, work and society, and energetic engagement in the cause of world mission.

Our ministry

- *Keswick: the event.* Every summer the town of Keswick hosts a three-week convention, which attracts some 15,000 Christians from the UK and around the world. The event provides Bible teaching for all ages, vibrant worship, a sense of unity across generations and denominations, and an inspirational call to serve Christ in the world. It caters for children of all ages and has a strong youth and young adult programme. And it all takes place in the beautiful Lake District – a perfect setting for rest, recreation and refreshment.

- *Keswick: the movement.* For 140 years the work of Keswick has impacted churches worldwide, and today the movement is underway throughout the UK, as well as in many parts of Europe, Asia, North America, Australia, Africa and the Caribbean. *Keswick Ministries* is committed to strengthening the network in the UK and beyond, through prayer, news, pioneering and co-operative activity.

- *Keswick resources.* *Keswick Ministries* produces a range of books and booklets based on the core foundations of Christian life and mission. It makes Bible teaching available through free access to mp3 downloads, and the sale of DVDs and CDs. It broadcasts online through Clayton TV and annual BBC Radio 4 services.

- *Keswick teaching and training.* In addition to the summer convention, *Keswick Ministries* is developing teaching and training events that will happen at other times of the year and in other places.

Our unity

The Keswick movement worldwide has adopted a key Pauline statement to describe its gospel inclusivity: 'for you are all one in Christ Jesus' (Galatians 3:28). *Keswick Ministries* works with evangelicals from a wide variety of church backgrounds, on the understanding that they share a commitment to the essential truths of the Christian faith as set out in our statement of belief.

Our contact details
T: 01768 780075
E: info@keswickministries.org
W: www.keswickministries.org
Mail: Keswick Ministries, Convention Centre, Skiddaw Street, Keswick CA12 4BY, England

Related titles from IVP

THE FOOD FOR THE JOURNEY SERIES

The Food for the Journey series offers daily devotionals from well-loved Bible teachers at the Keswick Convention in an ideal pocket-sized format – to accompany you wherever you go.

Available in the series

1 Thessalonians
Alec Motyer with Elizabeth McQuoid
978 1 78359 439 9

2 Timothy
Michael Baughen with Elizabeth McQuoid
978 1 78359 438 2

John 14 – 17
Simon Manchester with Elizabeth McQuoid
978 1 78359 495 5

James
Stuart Briscoe with Elizabeth McQuoid
978 1 78359 523 5

Ruth
Alistair Begg with Elizabeth McQuoid
978 1 78359 525 9

Praise for the series

'I was truly encouraged as I used this each day.' Peter Maiden, International Director Emeritus, Operation Mobilisation, and Minister-at-Large, Keswick Ministries

'These devotional guides are excellent tools.' John Risbridger, Chair of Keswick Ministries, and Minister and Team Leader, Above Bar Church, Southampton

'These bite-sized banquets . . . reveal our loving Father weaving the loose and messy ends of our everyday lives into his beautiful, eternal purposes in Christ.' Derek Burnside, Principal, Capernwray Bible School

Available from your local Christian bookshop or **www.ivpbooks.com**

Related Teaching CD Packs

James

Stuart Briscoe
SWP2239D (4-CD Pack)

John 14 – 17

Simon Manchester
SWP2238D (5-CD Pack)
SWP2238A (5-DVD Pack)

Also available

2 Timothy
Michael Baughen
(SWP2202D 4-CD Pack)

1 Thessalonians
Alec Motyer
(SWP2203D 5-CD Pack)

Available from www.essentialchristian.com